From the Eyes of a *Cowgirl*

R O B B I E   B U N K E R

ISBN: 978-1-7167-8031-8 (sc)
ISBN: 978-1-7167-8033-2 (hc)
ISBN: 978-1-7167-8030-1 (e)

Library of Congress Control Number: 2019919464

Lulu Publishing Services rev. date: 11/12/2020

From the Eyes
of a
Cowgirl

ROBBIE BUNKER

Table of Contents

Chapter 1   Jody Weimer, the Cowman 1

Chapter 2   The Earth Warms—Spring Roundup.................... 4

Chapter 3   Riding the Plateau—Summer............................. 29

Chapter 4   Task Masters 36

Chapter 5   The Working Crew 65

Chapter 6   Entertainment on a Budget 78

Chapter 7   Money Makers.. 82

Chapter 8   Money Makers..102

Chapter 9   The Buck Stops Here 108

Chapter 10   Cowboy Ingenuity... 118

Chapter 11   Drought and Fire 2018 134

Chapter 12   Where the Animals Live 142

Chapter 13   Family 164

I was the 101st child born in Uravan, a small town in Colorado. It is no longer in existence, but I am, and I carry on the values, beliefs, dreams, and American spirit of "get up and go."

I was a teacher in Los Angeles and moved back home to be with my mom; she was having difficulty remembering and eventually passed away from Alzheimer's disease. I was employed by the local school district and taught for eight years in the elementary school. The community is small and agriculturally based. When I lived in this western town, it was an agriculture and uranium-mining community, and agriculture, coal mining, and a power plant continue to help support the community. Soon our community will not have the coal mine or the power plant, due to government regulations.

In these pages, I hope you will find understanding and inspiration of the hard work it takes to keep America alive and united. I am one individual with hopes and dreams, not of one thought or one way but of the liberty to work hard, with dedication to my fellows. Get your hands dirty, be a part of the community, not just monetarily but with mind, body, and spirit.

I have always been a slight risk-taker, unafraid to try something new and a cheerleader for small town USA. I wrote this book to pass along my experience living in a different culture, the cowboy culture. Entering this new culture, I realized I needed to understand what they were talking about when they were sitting around the table, on a horse, or in a truck. The cowboy has a different language, so I began my little book of cowboy language to assist anyone with a preview of the cowboy's values, beliefs, and way of life. *The new vocabulary will be italicized and defined within the chapters.*

A note: when *the cowboy or The Cowman, TC,* is mentioned in the book, I am including women, children, and men in this identity. I want to be up front with the use of *cowboy* as an all-inclusive gender and age identification.

One afternoon after teaching, I was at the post office, sitting in my car, looking through my purse. I glanced over, and I thought I saw a friend of the family sitting in his truck. I took another look, and sure enough, it was Weimer. I got out of my car, and he motioned me over, calling out, "Come and look at this new critter." I walked over, and in his lap, sleeping was a white ball of fur. He woke this little critter up. Oh my, he was so cute; his puppy breath melted my heart. Haus was his name, a purebred border collie, the most common cattle dog in this area. The cowboy and I *shot the breeze,* talked, catching up on our families and gossip around town. He asked me for my number and said that he was moving cattle to the mountain. He wondered if I wanted to come up to the Club Cow Camp. I told him that I had one month of school left, and I would love to come up to cow camp. This was May 7, 2015.

Now I am on top of the world, learning and living in the "cowboy culture." It is a different world than I am used to. I grew up around the cowboys, but I would be called a *townie,* one who lives within the town. Now, you have to understand that the towns in the West are small, one thousand or less in population, and located approximately thirty to fifty miles from each other. I was told that this distance allowed our great-grandparents to travel by wagon or horse and have a resting place or a *watering hole,* drinking water. There were many farms and cattle ranches, but then you have the core of the town with a grocery store, post office, bank, gas station, liquor store, a saloon dance hall, doctor's office, school, and churches. This is the town; hence, I have always lived in town, so I am a townie.

In the summer of 2015, I started working at *The Club,* the cowboy's summer camp where the family graze their cattle. The cattle are taken to the Uncompahgre for grass and water so the winter range can rest and rejuvenate. After a few weeks I realized that I needed to understand the language; I was lost in translation. I needed to understand what they were talking about, either when sitting around the table or on a horse or riding in the truck. One afternoon when we were riding across a meadow into the trees to look for *stray cattle,* cattle not with the herd, the boss told me to go through the pine trees and to the pond and gather all *the slick calves* and bring them up to the meadow. In my head I was thinking, *I hope there are not too many, how will I gather them and what the heck did slick calves mean?* So, I was riding down through the trees to the pond and trying to put together what *slick* meant. Well, out in the world, slick means wet or shiny. I finally saw the calves; there were only five, thank goodness, but none of them were slick. So, I rode back to the meadow and told the boss that I found the calves, but none of them were wet or shiny. TC started laughing hysterically. He finally had to stop to catch his breath. With tears in his eyes, he told me slick means calves without a brand. Talk about a kind and forgiving boss! I began jotting down words and sayings so I could interpret what we were doing for the day or to understand what happened yesterday.

Knowing myself, I was bound and determined to understand what was going on. Besides, I was working with the cowboys, so I had better know what I was supposed to do. Knowing what to do was not only to be responsible but to fit in. Who doesn't want to fit in? Maybe just maybe the life I am privileged to live will give you a stepping-stone to finding your own or at least being aware that there are so many different cultures just waiting for you to explore or a willingness to understand.

*"Most social scientists today view culture as consisting primarily of the symbolic, ideational, and intangible aspects of human societies. The essence of a culture is not its artifacts, tools, or other tangible cultural elements but how the members of the group interpret, use, and perceive them. It is the values, symbols, interpretations, and perspectives that distinguish one people from another in modernized societies; it is not material objects and other tangible aspects of human societies. People within a culture usually interpret the meaning of symbols, artifacts, and behaviors in the same or in similar ways."** .*Banks, J.A., Banks, & McGee, C. A. (1989). *Multicultural Education.* Needham Heights, MA: Allyn & Bacon.

It is a privilege to be an American; coming to America and becoming a citizen does not mean losing our own culture but sharing our values, ideals, and the vision inherent in our own personal culture. Through sharing, we benefit the whole. With this ideal in mind, we will manage to come together, uniting our common goal, keeping a society that values freedom and individuality, honors difference of opinion and a common desire to support each other. United we stand.

I have always wanted to be a cowboy.

Chapter

Jody Weimer, the Cowman

The cowboy culture is one of passion, ingenuity, hard work, responsibility, and a life full of doing something you absolutely love. I am sure you have heard the cliché "working from sunup to sundown." Well, forget the sundown; it is, however long it takes to get 'er done. Cattlemen have a respect for the animals, the land, and a commitment to family and community.

When things are *edgeways*, topsy-turvy, and nothing seems to be going right and there is a glimmer of giving up, we *cowboy up*, look for different approaches and go forward. When we fall off a horse, we don't walk away; we get back in the saddle and try again. We don't shoot the horse or degrade the breed of horse. The cowboy experiences and assesses the situation. The cowboy accepts responsibility, searches to understand and learn from what happened. The cowboy knows the horse a little better and understanding helps him work with and learn from the event. This is called *resilience*, the ability to rebound. Building resilience is a learned behavior that increases our ability to rebound, to stick with our goals, our obligations, and move forward.

Responsibility, honor, respect, and communication are learned; they are not inherited. These values are taught and then practiced again and again. Such things as respecting our country, our presidency, our freedom, our teachers, parents, and individuals that make up this great country.

TC honors the forest, the grasses, the water, the animals, our country, and our way of life. When bad things happen, TC doesn't give up, doesn't dishonor or throw away something that isn't just perfect.

In 2018, TC was faced with a drought. The ranch had to sell part of their stock this year, but we don't deny that it is a drought; we work with it. TC doesn't give up; we keep our heads high, go forward, and breathe in the blessings and absorb the freedom that have been given us, and we *cowboy up*, move forward.

This year has been an awakening. Mother Nature reminded us that we are human. As the cowboy says, "Human beings are the only animal that thinks that it can control Mother Nature." We began 2018 with very little precipitation, no snow to speak of, which translates into no *snowpack*, snow built up from the winter. We rely on the snowpack for our summer water for communities, grasslands, forests, springs, farming, ranching, gardens, and aesthetic, such as lawns. The ranchers in the area depend on it for pasture and natural springs. Many ranchers had to truck water to their herds because the springs were dry.

This last year, a lightning strike ignited a tree at the base of the mountain. The fire was called in, and they said that they would get to it in a couple of days. When they "got to it" and found the fire, it had already burned five hundred acres. The Bureau of Land Management chose to let the fire burn, but it quickly moved on to the national forest. Now it is no longer a BLM fire but a National Forest Service fire. The forest was so dry, a jackrabbit had to pack a lunch; it had at least twenty years of dry, downed trees and debris. The fire consumed forty thousand acres of forest, but luckily, we received a large amount of rain in September, and it finally put out the fire. It was looking like we might have a normal snowfall that year.

Cowboy Up, America

Chapter

The Earth Warms—Spring Roundup

This is the time of the year when the cattle will be brought off the winter range. The spring roundup happens in late April through May. My excitement cannot be measured; I have a chance to awaken my inner cowgirl. (Remember, *I am working on the ranch, not just a bystander or guest.*)

The cattle are gathered in the spring to go to the top of the plateau, where they will spend June through November. Before going to greener pastures, the calves must be branded and the herd checked for any sickness or *slick calves*, calves that are not branded. Before branding, TC must gather the cows and bring them down from the winter range. We gather our friends and drive the Cowman's cattle off different wintering grounds. TC puts the cattle and calves in pens called *catches*. Then we go to *cutting*, separating the calves from their moms so they can be branded. Branding is a must if you want to keep your cattle and not let them end up in someone else's herd.

From the ranch, the horses have been caught, saddled, and put in the horse trailers. Going to one of the winter pastures is a time when TC will catch up with his friends, eat lunch, have a beer, and tell stories. When the destination is reached, the horses are unloaded from the trailer, and the cattle are gathered from the five-thousand-acre pasture and taken off the mountain. This is not done all in one day. Take a look at the view from the top of the mountain, where we have gathered the cows to go down to the bottom of the canyon.

Moving down the dirt road to the highway. Riding behind the cowboys to catch *the drive*, moving cattle from one area to another. The picture is a little blurred; I am on Governor, my horse. Generally, the cows are ready to go off the mountain; the feed can be a little sparse during the winter months, so hunger trumps attitude.

The cowboys have driven cows down and are waiting for the others to catch up. From here they will take the cattle up the highway. They are actually waiting for Loren and me; we had to take a bathroom break. We found the perfect spot, we thought, behind the bank of a man-made pond. No one could see us behind the fifteen-foot bank. So, off our horses we went; we took a squat, and out of nowhere we heard hooting and hollering. Three cows flew over our heads, then TC and Carl riding their horses flew over our heads, chasing the cows. We were still down in the squat position, our eyes wide open, pulling our pants up. Neither one of us could say a word.

Then we heard Carl yelling, "And that's a cow jumping over the moon."

Payback is a b----.

I was riding up on the herd, ready to encourage them down the road.

"Go out!" yelled TC. There were three *pairs,* three cows and three calves, trying to circle back up the mountain; the dogs will bring them back. The bikers had to maneuver themselves around the cattle. It is more difficult when you are going the same way the cattle are moving. If you are moving into the cows, they will go around the car or bike; all you have to do is stop or move very slowly. So breathe in and relax; you will find a time to move around in front of the cattle. Honestly, this is time well spent, waiting and watching. The calves are precious.

When traveling, these are the signs you will see to let you know to slow down and be alert. Other hints: when the sign says next thirty-four miles cows on the road, it is inevitable that you will not stay alert for thirty-four miles; pay attention to *cow patties,* cow poop on the road; then you will know that the cows are in the area, so slow down again. Remember, some cows are black; they are extremely hard to see at night. If the cow is facing the road, slow down. More than likely, she will cross the road, and her calf is not far behind. Calves are more unpredictable. If you see one cow, there are many. Since Colorado is an *open range state,* cattle are not fenced in and are allowed to roam on the highways. The driver is responsible for killing a cow on the road. Hitting a standing cow that weighs 1,250 pounds will absolutely damage your car. So slow down, breathe, and enjoy your travels.

The story goes, a federal government official in Washington ordered half of the cattle guards to be fired in Colorado due to the cost. Below is a picture of a cattle guard.

No one will be fired today; now that's a sad state of affairs.

Notice the cows and calves are moving off the road; behind them, the dogs are ready to *heel,* nip at the cow's heels, which moves them back into the herd.

TC will once again command the dogs to *"go way out,"* to gather the wanderers.

Love, Sweat, and Beer

Saddlebags are used to carry medicine for any sick cows and to carry our beer. A couple of beers on a hot day is not so bad, but they keep the medicine cool too.

Commands to the dogs will help the cowboy keep the wild ones in line.

The cattle are taken across the bottom of the canyon and herded to the other side. Tomorrow we will take the cattle up another dirt road to the corral or *catch,* where the calves will be branded. To repeat, this is not done in one day.

Back home, the horses, dogs, and friends will be fed. We will eat and laugh, the cowboys will embroider, a type of sewing craft that creates designs from thread, their stories while playing poker. This time is energizing. All day riding is tiring, but a gut full of warm homemade food, sharing those hilarious stories from the day and staying alert for cheating at cards will awaken anyone.

We gather our gear the next day, load the horses, and head to the catch, a fenced area we put the cows in yesterday afternoon. Up, up the canyon road to the next catch.

Herding the cattle over the top to the designated catch.

Without our horses and dogs, this would be an impossible task. When the cattle reach the top, they must be kept in a group to move them to the branding area. TC lets us know what our jobs are, and the experienced riders gather the stray cows back into the herd. The cattle usually stay in a bunch because the cows have their small calves with them. They are exceptional mothers and keep track of their calves by calling out for their calf, which alerts the calf where they are; the calf then calls back. At times the little calves tire and can get lost if the cowboy is not vigilant.

The cowboys will now round up the cattle and put them in the catch with their calves. They will have to throw their *lassos,* a stiff rope with a loop at the end, to catch the calves.

He throws a lasso like a pro, I think he just might be a pro.

In the beginning, fringe on the chaps was used to provide a cowboy with leather to mend a *bridle* or *reins,* devices used to control the horse.

Morgan is taking care of a calf that is too small to be branded.

Chow time. You gotta love hot dogs over an open fire.

Branded cows and calves heading to the plateau. An older lead cow will guide the herd. With her knowledge of the mountain, the others will follow.

Branding—Mesa Creek

Moving a different herd of cattle toward the catch above Mesa Creek.

Rounding up the cattle to put them into a catch to brand the calves. Not far up the road is called Sew 'Em Up Mesa. The story is, in the 1800s there was a gang of cattle rustlers stealing cattle in the area. They would take them back to their hide out and proceed to cut the brand off the stolen cattle and sew their own brand on.

Throwing the loop: a rope that has a loop in it and it is swung overhead and thrown out to catch a calf, cow, or bull. TC says if you have a lasso that never misses, never lend it to anyone; they will teach it bad habits.

Each cowboy in the catch will try to rope a calf, which is usually standing next to its mother. Once again you must realize just how protective these cows are of their calves. This is a twelve-year-old girl, and she is an excellent roper.

Bringing in a calf to be branded, vaccinated, and cut if it is a male. Can't have a herd of bulls; they would be fighting all the time.

The cowboy, Theresa, is keeping her horse quiet and back so the calf remains still while being branded.

Chapter

3

Riding the Plateau—Summer

The cattle outfit rides every day during the summer. We check on the herd for any sickness, missing cows, location of running springs, and watching for the poison in the pastures.

Waiting for the others to bring the cattle from another pasture and spinning some stories.

You are viewing this scene over my horse's ears.

All are ready at the gate.

Cowboy Dan can throw a loop. He is a friend of TC and volunteers his time to be on top of the world with his friends.

Our friends gather

Mother and son watching dad rope the calves. Mom is a cowboy too.

Doctoring any sick calves and castrating the male calves, called *steers*. *Rocky mountain oysters*, the testicles of small bulls, leaving them as steers. The dogs love them, but be aware, the oysters are extremely rich, and the dogs may not come into any cabin at night.

Branding calves

All done little doggie

Break time. The branding iron is hanging on the post, and the cowboy will be back at it after a snack, laughter, and some shade.

Cowboy rodeo, at the day's end. Ride 'em, cowboy. If you want to be a cowboy, you have to have heart.

Chapter

Task Masters

Dogs

Dogs are a must on any cattle ranch, especially if you are running cows on many acres. These dogs will keep the cattle in a bunch, so they will continue on the path that the cowboy wants them to. They are a special breed of dog, called *heelers,* trained to move the cattle by nipping at their heels. These dogs can work herding cattle from sunup to late afternoon. They are natural herders and often feel left out and pout if not working. We raise our puppies, which carry on the genetics and memory of the area that they are herding. Border collies, border kelpie, and border blue heelers/Catahoula gather cattle and can be trained to herd most anything. Heelers come from a long history of herding, dating back to Roman times. We occasionally will adopt new dogs from nearby ranchers. Picking the right dog is based on the relationship we have with ranchers in the area. They know their dogs and can choose a good heeler. Ranchers are a culture in themselves and work to create relationships and friendships passed down from generation to generation. As mentioned earlier, we carry on through the generations, helping each other any way we can.

Meet Paco

He was the best dog on the ranch. He could outrun and outmanuver any cow or calf. He followed commands automatically. His personality was charming, warm, caring, and he loved a good joke. You could tell by the smile that he showed you. I am not kidding; he smiled at me on many occasions. He was run over in December 2016. The cowboy is very stoic about death, but Paco was a different story. Rest in peace, old boy.

A lazy afternoon tending the cows and calves.

Meet Jack

You have to love him. Jack needs your attention all the time. "Pet me, please." He is a true border collie, loves to herd, and can go a whole day without complaining. Just let him find water to lie in, and he will go as far as you need him to. Although he is so dedicated to moving cattle, he has a second name: Jack Off. Now you might say, how dare you use that language, but just let me explain. When training a dog, you use simple commands like sit, down, or off. *Off* is a command used to let Jack know he has to get off the heels of the cattle and come back to the cowboy. So, Jack Off does not imply what you might think. Jack and Paco competed often, which caused him to inherit the command "Jack, off."

Since Paco's death, he is now the lead dog. He is very humble about his job. I am impressed by his change of purpose; he understands that he is now responsible to teach the other dogs what they need to do. Jack has earned another name, but I will tell the story at the end of this photo shoot of the leader, Jack.

Well, I promised to tell you about Jack's new name. We had left the dogs at camp while we ran to town to get mineral blocks for the cattle. When we returned, I noticed something black in the road in front of the cabin. The cowboy stopped the truck, and I opened the door as quickly as I could. Rounding the front of the truck, I could tell that it was Jack. He was lying on the ground, not moving. The cowboy told me to step back. I was already in tears. He knelt by Jack and listened for a heartbeat; he looked up and shook his head. I noticed blood was coming from his nose and head. The cowboy moved him—no heartbeat and a lot of blood. We carried him to the fire pit and left him there while we unloaded the mineral block in the barn. By the time we finished, the cowboy and I looked at each other and headed for the cabin. It had been a long day and devastating evening. We decided that we would take care of Jack in the morning. After having a bite to eat, I went outside. I knew I was going to cry. To my surprise, Jack was sitting at the door, just smiling. "Hey, cowboy, look who is at the door." "Well, I'll be, Come Back Jack," said the cowboy.

You've got to love that smile.

Meet Haus

Haus was the youngest of the three border collies. This is the puppy that lured me into the cowboy culture. After getting to know him and his owner, it was clear to me that Haus was in training, and I had a new life to live. I do not have many pictures of Haus as a puppy because I slipped in the creek, and of course my phone was in my back pocket. (The rice did not work.)

Even though I do not have pictures, I still have the memory of this pup looking to Paco and Jack for an education.

This young cowboy loves to ride and was one of Haus's favorite humans.

Meet Sam, the mixed breed

Blue heelers (American cattle dogs) are solid, sturdy, compact dogs with an alert, ready-to-work stance. They are often referred to as the Australian cattle dog. They're bred for driving cattle over long distances and across rough terrain. The hard-working Catahoula leopard dog, the official canine of Louisiana, was developed to catch wild hogs.

Sam is a blue heeler/Catahoula mix. As the information indicates, both dogs are herders. Sam is my dog, which the ranch inherited. The cowboy has been tolerant of Sam because he was a town dog, only loyal to me. Now, after three years, he works hard herding the cattle, keeping them in a bunch. He is called Hurricane because of his relentless circling. TC has been kind and patient with Sam, teaching him to go out and come back. Looks like the cowboy is teaching an old dog new tricks.

Fetch, Sam, Fetch

Bring it here, good boy. Too funny, no stick too big or small.

Sam says, "I'm not afraid."

A sniffing frenzy. "Okay, we're all in the truck. Let's move out."

Sam took care of this pup, but the eagle needed lunch. For a moment, my sadness restrained, I thought sometimes life is just not fair. A great opportunity to practice resilience.

The three amigos.

Robbie Bunker

Meet Mit-chel, the Australian Kelpie

An Australian cattle dog, or simply cattle dog, the kelpie is a breed of herding dog originally developed in Australia for driving cattle over long distances across rough terrain. Kelpies were created by crossing early collies with other herding dogs and possibly dingoes. The Australian kelpie can work stock for many hours and cover long distances in heat and dust without giving in. High intelligence means they learn quickly.

You could say her chest markings are in the shape of a steer or if you are from the city, Tesla.

I raised her and her three brothers. She is extremely affectionate and tends to focus her love on one owner—that would be me. Mit-chel can be stubborn but will succumb if she thinks you are angry. She often herds humans by nipping at the back of their heels, especially men.

When she was three months old, she *took to a cow,* herding instincts, when we were sorting cattle for market. Instinctually she started nipping at the heels of the calves, moving them down the lane. She was persistent and was kicked by a calf, breaking her jaw. She continued to eat and drink, so the cowboy thought she was going to heal just fine. She was out herding cattle the next day. I finally took her to the vet, and she was well in two weeks. Sometimes you must take them to a vet; that's the townie in me. The vet was an hour away, and it was snowing for the first-time last year, practically the only snow we got, which is rare. TC told us all that a drought is a-comin'.

This is a new puppy that Mit-chel took care of and taught the *ropes,* the ways of ranch life. His name was Gunner, and if you look closely, he is chewing on a very dried frog. Gunner's life was not an easy one. He was run over, and in a couple of days, he seemed to be okay. The cowboy took him to the mountain, in hopes that he wouldn't be run over again, but he became very ill and we lost him. It is tough living on a ranch.

"I went looking for the pot of gold," said Pete.

Canine Ninjas

There is always enough time to share a drink with a best friend.

Reach out and find community

Very timidly this puppy is seeking to befriend this new creature with the long, funny legs. Fear is natural. Assess the fear. Will I react with anger, discrimination, or confusion? Ruger was confused, too small to be angry, and thought, *so what if this dog is different?* Ruger decided it was safe to play with Yukon, the long-tailed, long-legged creature.

In a community, people will speak a different language or have a different culture or upbringing. It may take us a moment to understand or to know how to communicate with one another, but if we are open to learn new ideas and innovations, we just might make a new friend.

Ruger the puppy had such an experience with Yukon the hound dog. While playing in the yard with Yukon, Ruger tried to take Yukon's bone. Letting out a *bray,* a type of howl that only hound dogs can make, Ruger jumped straight in the air and started whining. Ruger got on his stomach and started crawling to Yukon. Ruger was unsure about what this creature was saying, he had never heard such a sound. After about ten minutes, Ruger walked up to Yukon and smelled her and decided she could be trusted. From that day forward, Yukon came every morning to take care of the puppies. It takes one of us to be adventurous and curious to make a difference.

Sharing cover from the rain.

Hmm, once again, getting along. Sometimes it is important just to step out of current thought and see the world through a full glass or a hungry belly. Maybe it wouldn't hurt some of us to want to understand instead of being understood

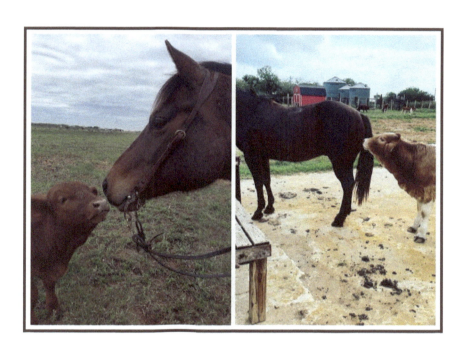

Be curious

Keep the faith. Love will conquer all.

I so agree.

Hank Davis, on the far left, celebrated their ranch's one hundredth year of family operation.

Father and son, what a wonderful experience to watch them listen, guide, and learn from each other.

Chapter

The Working Crew

The Quarter Horse

The American Quarter Horse, or quarter horse, is an American breed of horse that excels at sprinting short distances. Its name came from its ability to outdistance other horse breeds in races of a quarter mile or less; some have been clocked at speeds up to fifty-five miles per hour. The American Quarter Horse is the most popular ranch breed in the United States today, and the American Quarter Horse Association is the largest breed registry in the world.

Just a *foal*, a baby horse. They call me a *hay burner*; I had to laugh.
Horses do not work during the winter and are just fed, so they are
called hay burners.

Standing and waiting in undisturbed solitude and stillness.

Sh-sh-sh, no one knows I am free to roam. The Governor is a great horse; he will pack children all day and turn around the next day and herd cattle through the aspens at a full run.

I love people so much. They brush me, let me run like the wind, and always bring me home. I have very good eyesight. I can see behind me without turning my head; that's how well I see. Oh, I can also see at night, unlike the people who ride me. My sight was given to me because I have many predators that like to eat me—wolves, bobcats, lions, foxes, and bears.

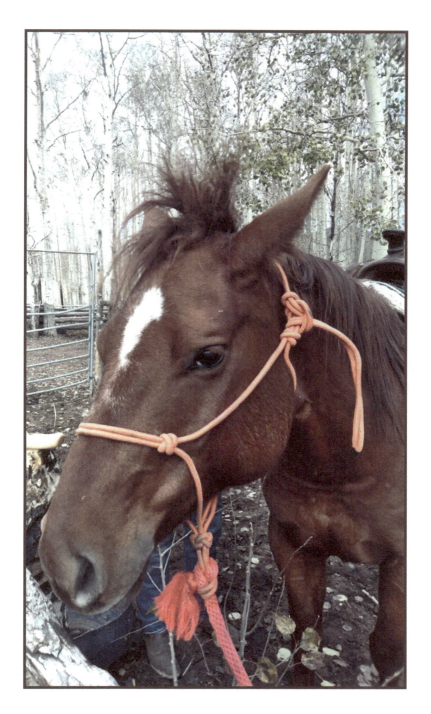

"Like my new hairdo?" Hey, big boy, my name is Cockle-Burr Abe.

The horses are ready for a long ride. A hunter has downed an elk, and the cowboys are going out to recover the elk. Our hunters come from all walks of life, from Tennessee, Alabama, Louisiana, Michigan, Missouri, Texas, California, Utah, and Arizona, and they are friends, people you can count on to help you in a pinch. They are friends who have their own cultures but come to Colorado for the cowboy way.

When this cowboy mounts his horse, you can almost feel his sense of freedom. This young man came to camp about eight years ago. He was eight when the cowboy took him in. Christian is an incredible cowboy. When we were riding together, he taught me how to read the hoofprints of the cows and calves. He showed me how to know if they were coming or going and if a calf was with the cow. Since we ride through the aspens, the oak brush, and search for watering holes, he taught me the different signs of predators. He trained me to notice different signs of predators, such as fur in the brush, bear marks on the trees, different *scat,* animal poop. If there was fresh scat, he readied himself to protect us. This is when the hair on the back of your neck prickles.

In the area on the mountain and in the low country, the land is riddled with rock. TC shoes the horses to prevent their hooves from cracking and breaking, which will usually bring a horse up lame. A lame horse cannot walk or run, which makes it unuseable to TC. The cowboy will shoe his horses at least every four months, depending on whether a horse has *thrown his shoe,* lost a shoe or wear and tear indicates new shoes. The territory that the cowboy travels means at least every two months. A well-to-do ranch will hire a farrier to shoe his horses at $90.00 a horse. If you have twenty horses at $90.00 a horse, that is $1,800.00 times six, making the grand total $10,800.00 a year. The cowman would rather shoe the horses himself and buy hay and oats instead. Oats are not cheap.

Tools needed for shoeing: Horseshoe, hammer, nail clenches (bends the nail), rasp (a very large nail file) and hoof nippers.

A rest for the horse's hoof. It is used to placing the hoof on top, so the cowboy can file the hoof. It is remarkably similar to filing our nails. But on the ranch, there is not any hoof polish, not yet. Besides, these horses are all *geldings,* neutered males.

On the ranch   On the mountain

The anvil and hammer are used to size the shoe for the horse. Each horse has a specific shoe size.

Using the rasp to file down the hoof.

Using the hoof nippers and a knife to clean out the hoof.

The cowboy, Toad, has already shaped the horseshoe on the anvil using the hammer. Every horse has a different hoof and walks differently on the shoe; this has to be taken into consideration. Toad is now hammering the nail into the shoe onto the hoof.

Jerry and Shelly love to ride and volunteer their time to help out the ranch. They shoe their own horses.

Picking up oats for the horses. Woman's work: boy can she maneuver this machine.

Chapter

Entertainment on a Budget

Just like in the movies.

Taking down a bull

Untying the bull

RUN

This is a common occurrence in town, the traffic jam. Moving cattle through town with our trusted horses and dogs.

Chapter

Money Makers

Save the Rainforest – Eat U.S. Beef

Cows come in all sizes, assorted colors, breeds, and calf-raising qualities. *Travelers* can travel six to ten miles to find water, round trip twelve to twenty miles in a day. Most cattle won't travel more than four miles to water. TC raises Beefmaster cattle and Black Angus. Beefmaster cattle are known for their strong mothering instincts, protectors of their young, and are travelers; they can travel quickly to water or food. This is especially important because they pasture on the Uncompahgre Plateau. Sometimes freshwater springs can be a journey, and there are many predators—mountain lions, bears, and coyotes.

Black Angus cattle are noted for their beef. So, do the math; when you mix these two breeds, you have a breed of cow that can care for their young, travel distances, and no matter what, they will find food and water. Oh, and by the way, the steaks, hamburger, roasts, and prime rib are incredible. Tender, moist, and just the right marbling, thanks to the Black Angus breed.

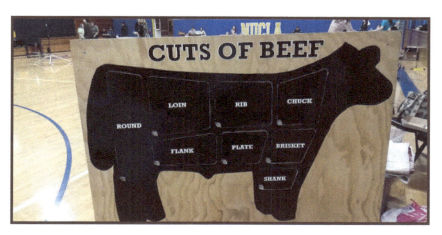

The Cattlewomen Association always do
agriculture presentations during job fairs.

I have come to respect these cattle for all those qualities and am impressed by their ability to find their way back to the mountain after being on winter pasture from December to May. TC recollects the time when they trucked the heifers and young calves to the top of the plateau. He said it seemed like a great idea, although his grandfather and father always herded the cows up the trails to the plateau. He thought he would get the cattle to the mountain faster than herding. Well, it ended up not being such a great idea, because they did not know how to go down to the lower country. They did not have the experience of traveling. We all need to experience life so we can find our way through and find what is meaningful to us.

Stomps are places where salt is put out for the cattle.

Heading to place salt out for the cattle. It is a crisp morning, blue skies, flowers everywhere. You can see forever, and there is not another vehicle on the road. We were carrying twelve blocks of salt at forty pounds each in the back of the truck. Some of the pastures were too far off the road, and the salt must be carried by horseback.

Cows can smell the salt; I happen to glance back, and there are at least fifty cows following the truck. The cattle need salt to stay healthy. TC purchases salt blocks that are full of minerals to help protect them from a poisonous plant called larkspur. This plant grows wild on the plateau, and when eaten by the cow, their blood congeals, and their hearts can no longer pump the blood. TC told me if he can catch the cow early enough, he might be able to save her by making her bleed. He has cut off ears and tails and has been successful. However, finding the cow early enough, over 100,000 acres, is rare.

"Cattle act as upcyclers in our food system—they upgrade plants into high-quality protein for people—beef, livestock, especially ruminants like beef cattle, play a key role in sustainable food system. A ruminant is an animal with four compartments in its stomach. Cattle allow us to produce food on marginal lands that are unsuitable for cultivated agriculture, such as fruit or vegetable production.

"Cattle eat grasses grown on marginal lands and other forage crops, like alfalfa. Marginal lands are those that are too rocky, steep and/or arid to support cultivated agriculture. Globally, livestock also eat over 1.9 billion metric tons of leftovers from human food, fiber, and biofuel production." www.GrowingYourFuture.com

Bulls

Everyone on the ranch has experienced this bull, Not Very Nice. This bad boy has been roped at least one time by every cowboy on the ranch. This bull protects his herd from other bulls; the fight is on.

Bulls are fertile male cattle that love the cows during their heat cycle but couldn't care less about the herd when they are not hot.

"All right, you really want a piece of this?"

The ranch purchase Beefmaster and Black Angus bulls. TC has made a special relationship with both families they buy bulls from. TC is passionate about keeping friendships and working relationships; he takes time to visit and share his life and being a part of theirs. I have gone on the bull-buying trips, and the families are passionate and gracious.

This is the one thing that we are missing in our lives today. Take time to visit a friend, notice the life around you, pause, take a moment just to pay attention. Let the moment in, and smile.

Winter on the Ranch

Every morning the house is full of cowboys and farmers, sitting around the table, touching base with each other on anything that happened yesterday and planning the day. Politics and some gossip always enlivens the crew. Oh, and practical jokes and humor are constantly on the menu.

We are assigned our jobs, and we proceed to put on our boots, coats, and hats, and out the door we go. Feeding takes place right after the morning meeting. Each cow pasture needs to be checked, ice broken in the ponds and watering tanks, liquid protein put out, fences mended, heifers checked every two hours, the nursery cleaned, and orphan calves checked on.

The truck has dropped off the hay for the morning. TC in the pickup is checking the herd for any sickness.

She's off to have a calf

Breaking ice in the winter

Heifers are two-year-old cattle. They are female and have been mated with a bull. Heifers are the livelihood of the herd. They are watched very closely during the months of February and March. This is the time they will be having a calf, sometimes two, but rarely. A *heiferette* is a heifer three to four years old with a little more experience birthing and raising their young.

Heifers are watched very carefully during this time. We help the heifers with their first birth. Out in the pasture, they are identified by full, tight bags, and when they are close to having the calf, they are put into a corral next to the house.

Identification of a cow or heifer going into the birthing pose. Hint: The cow or heifer will have a tight bag, and her tail will be straight out and look like the handle on a pump. Once again, experience is at play.

This is an older cow; notice the tail looks like a pump handle, the tight bag, and even the calf coming out of the cow (looks like a big balloon).

During the three months of calving, a chair is the best bed. We take turns during the evening and early morning. If I have early morning, 12:00 a.m. to 4:00 a.m., I will sleep in the recliner and have an alarm set for every two hours. If TC has early-morning shift, he doesn't need an alarm; his personal alarm goes off. When on heifer duty, TC is looking for a heifer that has a tight *bag*, large udders full to bursting with milk, not chewing her *cud*, bringing chewed food back into her mouth to be chewed again, and usually lying down. Always take a spotlight with you.

During calving, these new mothers can have difficulties. The new calf may be turned the wrong way, may be born with the sac still intact, or may need to be pulled from the heifer, so it will not suffocate, or they may be doing just fine, like the heifer in the picture. This heifer is doing just fine; that's the baby coming out. What you are seeing is the amniotic sac; sometimes, the sac is too thick and needs to be broken before the calf suffocates. The sac is usually torn, or the heifer will lick the calf so the sac will break. If the sac is too thick, the cowboy has to break it so the calf will breathe air. When the cow drops the calf, the umbilical cord is broken. There have been times when the cord has been broken off at the calf's stomach. When this happens, the stomach must be sewn up. If TC doesn't find it in time, the calf will bleed to death. Vigilance is our motto.

Miracle of Three Minutes

The calf will be up and standing within three minutes. If the calf is born in the middle of the night, they will be herded into the nursery. It will be easier to check on the newborn and keep the heifer and calf warm.

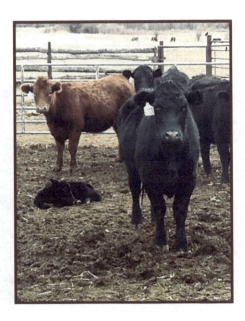

Don't you dare get any closer! Look into her eyes, narrow and menacing. Now, that is one serious heifer.

The Nursery

There are times when a heifer will not let a calf suck because she doesn't know that she is a mother. She will not claim her own calf. The cowboy will try to find another heifer or a cow that has lost its calf and try to *pair them,* put them together. A hide of the lost calf will be placed on the abandoned calf, which will mimic the smell of the calf lost. The new mother will usually go to the calf and take it for her own.

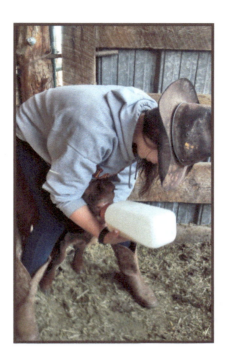

This bottle baby has to be fed in the morning, checked in the afternoon, and fed again at 5:00 p.m. and checked at 8:00 p.m.

He's doing great. After three feedings, you become the calf's surrogate mother. The elation and feeling of responsibility raise you to a new warming in the center of your chest. So, every morning you are greeted by this calf followed and butted until you have the bottle ready for it to suckle.

This cow is babysitting eleven calves while the other cows are out eating. If I get any closer, the cow will start getting the calves up, and the mother cows and heifers will come running.

Texas Beefmaster cattle

Chapter

8

Money Makers

Initially, the cows are *preg tested,* checking to see if they are carrying a calf. *Cull,* cows that have not conceived or are old, will usually be sent to the *sale barn,* a business where livestock is sold.

First, the tail is lifted. Then an arm is inserted into the anus. TC is determining when the cow will be giving birth. An experienced rancher can check for the first, second, and third trimester.

Sorting and shipping the steers and heifers for sale. Calves are sorted from their mothers. They are sorted for any illness, injuries, weight, brand, and gender.

The calves are driven down the lane.

Then the calves are put on a semi. The semi is driven to the coal plant and weighed. They use the plant's scale because it is certified.

The weigh station at the power plant. The ranch uses this station to weigh the trucks loaded with heifers and steers. The semi-truck is weighed first and driven to the ranch to get the load of steers and heifers. Then the load is weighed again to calculate the total weight of the steers or heifers.

Chapter

9

The Buck Stops Here

Sale Barn

TC has cultivated many relationships over the years with his honesty, generosity, and a strong belief in his cattle. With *cashmere,* smooth dealing, TC has developed relationships with cattle buyers, neighboring ranches, and the owners of the sale barns.

TC took me to the cattle sale one hot autumn day, and the flies were having a fiesta on my head. The auctioneer started the sale. He spoke so fast; I had some difficulty understanding him. This was my first auction. I was sitting next to the boss, and the flies were driving me crazy. I started swatting at them to keep them away from my face. Finally, Dan said, "Weimer, is your friend bidding on your cattle?" swatting flies had indicated that I was bidding. The whole place laughed, and I stopped swatting. Oh, my!

That morning in the sale barn, many cowmen were bidding on a *lot of calves,* a group of calves. During the auction, I noticed bidders on their phones, watching the computer bids on the monitor, and cowmen in the stands bidding. The bottom line is how much did that group of calves weigh and what was the price per pound.

There is a horse auction every first Saturday of every month. When a horse is ridden into the barn, it has a better chance of making more money. Showing how the horse is trained is a plus.

 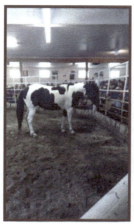 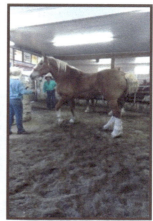

Toad—his real name is Jody—just rode his horse through and is showing the bidders how well trained the horse is.

Other Livestock

Cortez is very close to the Navajo and the Ute reservation. They are ranchers and farmers.

THE AUCTION WITH T

TC struck up a conversation with this gentleman for the entire sale. He has his father's ranch and is trying to make a living like the rest of us.

South Texas

One morning in Pearsall, Texas, we were sitting out on the porch having our coffee, and Dever said, "Hey, let's go to the Beef Master Sale." Patsy and Dever raise Beef Master too. I am always ready for an adventure. We were in the sale barn, and we decided to have a little lunch. We went to the kitchen, which had a Texas barbecue. We sat down at the long table with benches. I struck up a conversation with the gentleman across from me. He asked me where I was from; I told him Nucla, Colorado, and he said, "You wouldn't happen to know the Weimers?" To my amazement, he had sold Beef Master Bulls to TC's mother, May Weimer. It is such a small world; if you're neighborly, you will be amazed at how many people you know.

To love and care makes staying in the moment easier. Tony and Dustie operate the family ranch, WW McKinley, Inc. Beefmaster.

Teaching a new skill and hoping the boy will be resilient; to come back tomorrow. When I learn something new, I judge myself endlessly. I go over my mistakes, with judgment, I tell myself I could have been better. So I recognize the judgment and let it fly away. I am not perfect and will never be.

The neighbor's longhorn

Chapter

9

Cowboy Ingenuity

To be successful, the cowboy wears many different hats to continue a family legacy. Let us look at just a few of the hats they wear to keep the ranch.

Carpenter

We moved a cabin from the lower winter ranch to the summer camp. Why didn't they just build a new one, you might ask? It has been in the family for over sixty years. Keeping in touch with memories is better than a photo album.

Jerry, my brother, and TC were building a back porch on the cabin.

TC built these cabins with the help of friends.

This building is the saloon, and I believe it is at least seventy years old.

Building a porch for his home at the ranch which he and his son built, they laid 10,000 brick, hard work and determination.

Fencing Crew

Sam and Trevor have been building fence for TC since 2006. Both young upstarts have grown their business into one of the most sought-after fence builders in the area. When you speak of genuine people, these two come to mind immediately.

Cowboy ingenuity: TC uses his truck to string an electric fence, which contains the cattle in temporary pastures.

Before Trixie, the *mare,* a female horse, became pregnant, she had injured her left front leg. She was not going to recover, but the cowboy wanted her to have the *foal,* a baby horse, so Theresa and Dan, the cowboys, came up with a fix to allow her time to have her foal. Dan crafted a small ski-like shoe out of iron to keep her bowed tendon stable. She was able to carry Jema, the foal, to term. Now that's cowboy ingenuity.

Welding

Welding is a great skill to have for building fences, gates, small brackets, gate locks, and vehicle repair. Little Jody, TC's son, was building his own cabin.

Mechanic/Equipment Operator

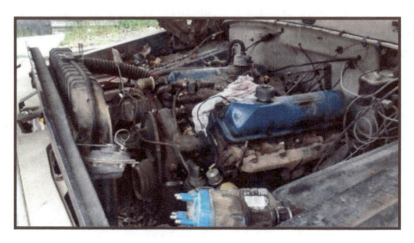

If TC has the part, they can fix it.

Solar power is used to charge the battery on Old Major, the tractor. Solar energy gives lights for the main cabin; the batteries store the sun's power from the solar panels.

When I first started working at the cow camp, the cabins had gas lamps. I truly like gas lamps better. They glowed a soft light and helped me wind down the day.

TC is clearing the old-growth away from the cabins for fire safety. The dozer is used to remove the road to the cow camp.

Jerry, my brother, was here from California and operated Old Major. He told me that we had the same backhoe forty years ago. They don't make them like they used to. Nor are they maintained and valued. If a part can be found: Old Major will continue to run.

A new, not used but new, side-by-side. This unit is handy when it is raining, snowing, or you have an injured or abandoned calf. TC has used it to pull cows and calves out of ponds or streams when they have gotten stuck in the mud and could not get themselves out. TC has also used it to carry calves back to camp to heal them back to health. It's quite a useful rig.

The baby calf is with her mother and will bounce back-resilience.

Animal doctors

Vaccination day

Spraying the cows for worms and any other small pests.

He is filling liquid protein tanks for the cattle. The protein helps balance their diet during nursing.

Yes, people still use chains

Household

The largest meal is around seven in the evening. We all chip in, and there is always a large quantity of food prepared, just in case we have friends drop in. Favorite foods include beans, roast beef with mushroom soup (cooking in cast iron pots all day), tacos, enchiladas, steak, hamburgers, and always potatoes. If you want Weimer to share his recipes, (pronounced "rekipe," with a long *i*), you're gonna have to ask.

We had a long day, continually moving cattle away from pastures that are in danger of burning. The drought and fire had us on the run for the months of August and September. Most likely, the conversation was about what the firefighters told us, and the forty-three years of experience TC has. Sometimes talking to the Forest Service about the grasses, the springs, and wildlife is like reading a newspaper with no print.

Hunting Season

One night after dinner, we were talking about all the bears we have seen in our lives. Brad and his dad told us a story about tracking a bear in the forest, and they noticed that they were tracking the bear in a circle, or maybe the bear was tracking them. Brad shot into the air to scare the bear. Looking through the gun scope, across the draw, he located the bear. The bear was sitting on the hillside, looking at Brad. Brad took down his gun and raised it to take another look, and through the scope, he saw the bear pull the oak brush in front of himself as if hiding.

Every cabin is cleaned after visitors leave and laundry washed. I always keep a pair of binoculars on hand. There are mountain lions and bears that come into camp.

We were driving to the Salvation Army when I spilled coffee down my shirt. We walked in, and Houston went to the jeans rack, and I went to pick out a shirt. After washing my original shirt and putting on the shirt I bought, we got in the truck and headed to the sale barn. I told Houston to put my wet shirt on the hanger and put it out the window. Hence the lingo "cowboy laundry" was given a place in cowboy language.

Chapter

10

Drought and Fire 2018

TC knew in January 2018 that there was going to be a severe drought this year. These are the only pictures I have in January. The Club is usually under five feet of snow.

Spring 2018. Looking for water, TC walked across the common watering hole. He did find mud, but this pasture will not sustain the cattle.

Spring Creek 2017, Spring Creek 2018

Spring Creek 2017—this pasture is used to feed the cattle before they move to the plateau. After the cattle move onward to the plateau, the meadows are irrigated. The picture on the right is the pasture in 2018.

The Tongue 2017   The Tongue 2018

July 2008—The fire was started by a lightning strike in late July. It moved very quickly through the BLM, the Bureau of Land Management, and when the firefighters could not stop it, the fire moved very quickly up the mountains toward the plateau.

The fire was traveling fast, and we were able to see the hot spots at this distance. TC was over in the *draw,* where two hills or mountains join at the base where the creek runs, gathering cattle when he heard a whoosh, and he knew he had to get out of there fast. The flames were igniting the pines, and flames were jumping from tree to tree. Pines give off *pitch,* the sap that runs out of this type of tree, that is very flammable. The next morning, he went back to the same area, looking for cattle, and he came across a *culvert,* a pipe in the ground to carry water. The fire had jumped so fast last evening because it had traveled through the pipe to the other side of the draw.

The next morning, we went down the mountain to the Delta Sale Barn for the horse sale. The crew was at the sale barn. The place was packed, and there were quarter horses for sale. Suddenly, our group started picking up their phones. Sam told the cowboy, "We have to go; the fire is on The Tongue." *The Tongue* looks like a tongue when you say *ah-ah*. This landform has deep drop-offs on three sides and is about five football fields from the cow camp. We were approximately an hour and a half away from the camp. When we arrived at the camp, our friends helped us load the horses and *tack,* saddles, pads, reins, and halters. We are fortunate to have such good friends.

The Tongue, 2019, all three sides were burned.

Look just left of the center, and the roof of the cabin is in plain sight, the silver object. The Club was very close to the approaching fire (2019).

The Club Cow Camp

After the forest service cleared the trees away from camp, I felt safer in camp.

Chapter

11

Where the Animals Live

The deer know where to stay in town. At least there is a little food and water. In the evening, there are at least twenty does in my neighbor's yard. One evening, coming home from work, I drove into my lane and parked. I glanced over the fence and saw all these does lying down, sunning themselves. I love being in the wild, wild West.

Look closely at the antlers on this young buck; they are in velvet. Each year, the male will grow new antlers. When they are in velvet, the antlers are growing. Toward the approaching summer, they will use trees or rocks to rub the velvet off. Then they have these beautiful antlers.

This is a bull elk, and they have antlers too; he has already rubbed off the velvet.

The picture is showing *Cow elk,* a female elk. The elk move off the plateau for winter to the ranchers' fields.

Where the *bars*, bears, are. We saw a mother bear and her three cubs down in this draw.

Scat, bar poop.

Bar paw print: actually,
bars are all over the plateau.

There are brown, cinnamon, black, and the most unique one I have seen was a cream-colored bear with brown paws. It is important to know what the bear eats, so you are not standing in a grove of gooseberries. They eat pinon nuts, gooseberries, rosehips, acorns, dead animals, and live animals. The ranchers dread the bear because the loss of calves is costly. A cow will protect her young; however, if a bear claws the calf, they usually do not live for long. A bear bite or gash will infect the calf. Bears are incredibly filthy, and the infection can be lethal.

The plateau and town are full of animals large and small. There are chipmunks, porcupines, squirrels, coyotes, badgers, bobtails, *putty tats,* which are mountain lions, hawks, eagles, cranes, turkey, *chickens,* which are actually grouse, numerous birds, elk, deer, red fox, river otter, muskrat, mice, raccoons, and *raggits,* which are rabbits. When riding a horse or in the truck, I have seen all these animals. But for some reason, they don't stop to pose.

Bucks, male deer   Albino raccoon

Chipmunk in his living room.   Lucky, the feral cat

Colorado Rocky Mountain Big Horn Sheep

I had an epiphany. I don't have to do this on my own.

What do you see?

What do you see?   What I see, a forest dragon.

Wild turkeys in the springtime.

They were dancing to the new day.　　Nothing is meaningless.

Geese on their long trek north, you've got to do what you've got to do.

Natural springs are ever dripping, but in the spring thaw, it will run full-on. Don't postpone your life; we are given one life and one lifespan.

Running down through the canyons to deliver life.

This corral was used to ship cattle by truck.

Heading up to the camp, bringing groceries and more blankets, I saw a putty tat zipping across the road in front of me. It is so exciting to see wild animals; they are beautiful and full of life. They live each day and only that day. There is a sense of peace living in the present.

This cabin was built in the 1800s. The cabin was built using hand-hewn wood, a hand-dug well off to the side, and a cellar to the left of this picture. The cattlemen ran about seven thousand cattle on the plateau in the 1800s. It was burned this summer in the fire.

She stands on her own, surrounded by protection from above.

The oak brush was so thick, and no water for miles; TC said that the raggit had to pack a lunch and water just to make it to the *park,* a flat, grassy area.

Snowpack

This must be what heaven looks like.

Readying for winter

Breathe in and breathe out. Open yourself to wonder.

We are searching for stray cows and calves. When we locate them, we will go back to camp and saddle the horses.

Nature gives us the opportunity to practice resilience.

Winters like these are exactly why towns were stitched together for survival.

I shall be true because there are those who trust me.

Chapter

Family

Last but not least is family. My definition of family is a group of people who are there for you in times of need and happiness; they would give the shirt off their back if you asked.

My family encouraged all of us to go to college, get a degree, and seek a profession. They encouraged us to be independent and successful. My father's family came from Oklahoma. During the Depression, my grandmother cleaned rooms and did whatever needed to be done. She raised four children during these hard times, and the children worked at any odd job to help buy food and some clothing. She washed the prostitutes' clothing and bedding and cleaned their cabins. She always told me that you never speak badly about someone until you have walked in their shoes. The ladies would always bring whatever extra food they might have and drop it off on the doorstep. My father, his brothers, and sister honored and respected my grandmother. My mother was from Austin, Texas. Grandpa was a well-known roofer. He was contracted to put the roof on top of the Texas Capitol. My grandmother raised cattle, horses, and pigs and hunted. She grew a huge garden and raised three children and four grandchildren. My family believed in America and valued a job and opportunities.

The saying, don't judge until you have walked in another's shoes, can help us in any generation. I am always impressed by how our society can get along with so many different perceptions of life. Sadly, in our society today, people from all walks of life are not free to express their opinions or experiences. If you have a different view than the teachers or mainstream media, you are put into a category of uncultured deplorable and not worthy of an opinion. This elitism saddens me greatly, but I will not choose to be a victim. I voice my opinion and listen to others. I'm not scared.

Grandma Bunker and my son Robert

Grandma Little with her kill: a rattlesnake, Havalina pig, and a buck. She was an inspiration; letting me know I could do anything.

The Bunkers

Mother and daughter

Dad is teaching me how to be a leader. Dad was a Ninety-Day Wonder in World War II. These men were trained in ninety days to fly and go to war.

Laura Snyder (Debby's daughter), Robert (my son), and Brittany Cecile (my daughter)

Brittany and Robert

When my father retired, he decided he wanted to build a cattle herd, so my family started *learning the ropes*, the ins, and outs of a new job, ranching. I was utterly excited about this adventure.

Both of my parents are deceased, but my nephew and niece's families are in ranching, and their children are being raised in the agricultural arena. The following is a snapshot of family and friends.

Monte was married to my sister, Debby; she had breast cancer and passed away. They have two children, Lothan and Laura. Lothan and Regan have two beautiful girls, Shay and Hadley. Laura and Andy also have two incredible children, Kannon and Chloe. The families have a vested interest in the community, just as my parents and Mex and Phyllis have. Our families live to carry on a family legacy and support the town.

Debby was my balance in life. She had compassion and joy and lived one day at a time; she was Mother Earth. I miss her presence here on Earth, but I find comfort knowing she is my angel, and I ask for guidance every day.

Debby and Monte Snyder

Grandpa Mont, Chloe, and Hadley, the little ones

Shay and Regan

Hum-m-m

Horsemanship

Kannon and Laura

Mom is the greatest teacher ever.

Shay, showing her steer at the county fair. The county fair is the oldest form of a community celebration in small-town USA. Children participate in 4-H to develop citizenship, leadership, responsibility, and life skills through experience. The parents love these skills; the kids just like hanging out with their friends and competing.

From the top, left to right:

Hadley, Chloe, Shay, Hadley

Bottom left: Shay and Grandpa Monte Snyder

Bottom right: Andy, Chloe's dad, Chloe, Hadley and the steer they raised

Christian, Wyatt, and Kindle

Weimer's playing around

Gabe loving Jack

The cowman's daughter and grandchildren, Hanna, in the cheer outfit, practicing for Nationals; the tournament was in the Los Angeles area, and they placed second. On the right are Haley and her brother at her graduation party.

Left to right

Amy, Hanna, Kasey, and Haley

Amy has raised three successful, smart, go-getters all on her own. Amy is successful in her career and an accomplished horseman.

Friends up the valley

When our team is playing away from home, and we get a bad call, we cry out *home cooking,* like cooking the books.

Hey, look, they are alive without a cell phone.

These are just a few of the young men TC has taken in to help them experience a feeling of purpose, pride in themselves through accomplishment and camaraderie. One young man was doing community service, and the younger ones are from the Denver area.

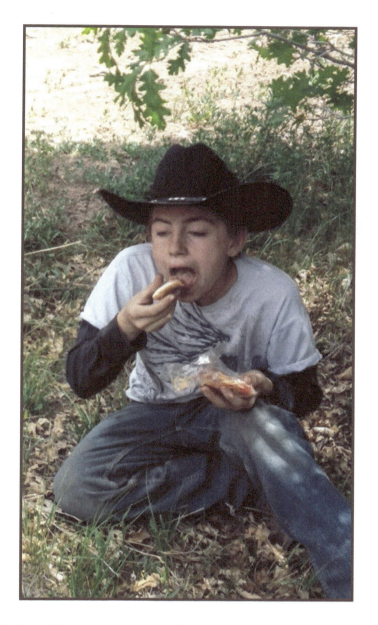

Say hello to Houston. He comes from the Denver area but is eager to know the cowboy way. We know how important it is to bring a lunch and lots of water. When the cowboy says we will be gone a couple of hours, it will never happen. This couple-hour trip took six hours. Always be prepared.

What an incredible day. We had barbecue, beer, meeting up with friends, and cowboy competitions. The best competition was the donkey race. There are four teams of two people and a donkey. They must go through an obstacle course, leading or riding their donkeys. In the final part of the race, every contestant rides the donkey, or however, they can put the donkey plus themselves in a very large horse trailer. When everyone is in the enclosed trailer, the side door is opened, and the team that gets out first and crosses the finish line wins. If you have any knowledge of donkeys, they are a stubborn lot. I mean stubborn. They go when they want to, they buck, run, and do not like to be ordered to do much of anything, especially when they don't know you.

At the party, we met four bicyclists who were riding across the Uncompahgre to Moab, about a three-day ride. They were from Europe and California, just a great group. TC paid for the entry into the donkey race for one of our newfound friends. He was from Spain and went for it with one of our hired hands. It was a great race, and they ended up winning. It was hysterical.

We come together to celebrate life.

Rest in peace, Ted

Rest in peace, Dewey

Buck Galley's Funeral

Buck was one of the original true cowboys when I was growing up. His mother, Mrs. Galley, was my sisters' teacher and a great teacher she was. Times are changing, and this book reflects what is still here but fading away, the true rural Americans and their families. The glue that holds us together.

Standing at the cemetery, looking out over the town, the bare trees with a hint of snow glistening in the light reflected off the ground snow. The air is crisp, a tiny nip at your skin. Tears filled my eyes, thinking about all the times as a child, we rode the horses and our bikes without fear. The only possible fear was not getting back to the house in time for dinner. We had a place in the world that gave us joy and warmth, and I fit in. These golden times paved our way to health, honor, respect, and happiness if we were willing to accept these gifts.

Planting the Seed

I have always been a cheerleader. I hold precious the men and women of this nation that work tirelessly, keeping the thread of society strong with hard work, determination, tenaciously solve challenges to keep the fibers of this great country intact. We are the heart and soul of the dream.

It is what it is, the great teacher. Now what we do with the lesson is another step we must take.